105 Tips For Creating An Emotionally Intelligent Organization

More Success By Focusing On Work Attitude And Motivation

Edited by
Patrick Merlevede & Gary Vurnum

105 Tips For Creating An Emotionally Intelligent Organization: More Success By Focusing On Work Attitude And Motivation

ISBN: 1456587765
EAN-13: 9781456587765

For author contact information, go to: **www.merlevede.biz**

Foreword

Daniel Goleman started a movement with his work in Emotional Intelligence. We can no longer find any justification for ignoring people's needs. However the demands on people at work have increased exponentially as technology has allowed us to complete tasks ever quicker with ever more complexity. And we now live in a global economy that is extremely volatile. The result is many people are more highly stressed than they have ever been and they are suffering from deep feelings of insecurity about their work, their personal life, their productivity, work-life balance etc.

For organizations to be effective under these conditions, we need to be particularly sensitive to all our stakeholders needs. In 2009 I became the president of the Canadian Association of Professional Speakers. It was my task to run that disparate organization of free spirits and independent people. As I prepared to take on the responsibility I decided that I would create an environment on the Board of Directors that will be the most fun and the most productive experience that anyone has ever had up to that time. Why wouldn't I? Why wouldn't anyone take on a mission of this sort? Why wouldn't you make this the absolute best experience for you people that it can be and enjoy the ride? Why wouldn't you want all the members of your team to have the time of their life working with you?

105 Tips For Creating An Emotionally Intelligent Organization: More Success By Focusing On Work Attitude And Motivation gives you ideas, hints, and inspiration to help you do just that.

The authors from around the world are experienced practitioners who have many years' experience in bringing out the best in people. And even if you are working in a stressed-filled environment, most people can find time for tips -- thoughts that help you improve what you do and how you do it. There are also thought-provoking questions to ask yourself – to make your work & your life more intentional.

Check out this book for yourself, allow yourself to think about those tips that relate to your present challenges and I suspect you will find some very useful advice.

Enjoy.

Shelle Rose Charvet,
author of *Words That Change Minds* and
The Customer is Bothering Me.

Introduction

An emotionally intelligent organization is a workplace where people's emotions are taken into account. Where there is empathy in the sense that people understand what is important to others, and know how their colleagues are motivated, like to organize their work and get a chance to do the work they like doing, maximizing their strengths.

Maybe this sounds idealistic and difficult to you. We beg to differ.

The authors of book have come together to give you practical tips of how it can be done. Each of the authors of this book works as trainer, consultant or coach to create more emotional intelligent workplaces.

You will learn how simple ideas can make a huge difference in all aspect of what tends to be called "human resources management": recruiting, training, coaching, managing, building teams, handling conflicts, retention, and even outplacement.

How To Use This Book

"The value of an idea lies in the using of it."
- Thomas A. Edison

This book can be used as an action guide to create a more Emotional Intelligent working place. Even if you just set aside 15 minutes each day for one of the tips, and you follow through, you can create some tremendous improvements in a couple of month's time.

Each of the tips of this book requires less than 1 minute reading. Use the other 14 minutes to consider how it applies to you and your work environment.

Ask yourself:

"What can I do today, to act on this tip?"

Remember, often it's just small differences, or small actions which create a huge difference!

Contents Of The Book

The tips are arranged by category. In the first series of tips we are following the employee along the path through the organization: from attracting the right candidates to the moment that people are leaving the organization.

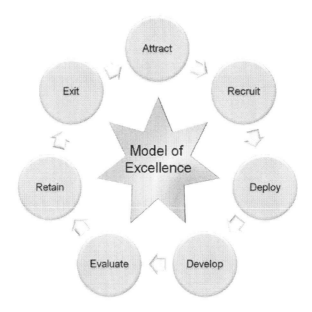

The remaining tips deal with topics, such as Organizational Culture, Team Building, Managing A Team and Mergers & Acquisitions.

Attract

Talent is not always enough.

1

We know success isn't always about ability, so why do we still behave like it is? The best performers at work are not always better educated, smarter, or even more experienced than the rest, but they usually have a 'way of being' that just works in their role. It is motivational alignment which equals true job fit. Find it, hire it and all will reap the rewards.

Attract

Describe the role in your job adverts by explaining the behaviors that will be expected.

2

This may sound odd but it means that only people who identify with those behaviors will be attracted to the role. You may get fewer applications but the quality will be better.

Attract

Embed objective information about work attitude and motivation in your job description.

3

Many job ads seem to be asking for people with a combination of qualifications that doesn't exist or is rare to find. Make the job description more real by describing what seems to motivate the top performers. Ask the question to the people really doing the job, and performing well. What motivates them? What do they see as positive challenges? What do they like most about their jobs? What's the difference between them and people which don't last long in that job role?

Attract

Make your job ads stand out.

4

Many job descriptions consist of a list of bullet points of what is required from a good candidate. Consider writing a story instead, what happens during a week in the job? What does it look like? If working with people is important, consider adding pictures of real people doing the job. Or insert other pictures showing the reality of the job. Maybe you want to add a testimonial of one of the top performers. Sometimes a couple of web pages on your site can help candidates to get a real feel what the job will be like.

Recruit

Know the behaviors required for success in the role.

5

It is important to have a job description as part of the recruitment process but many people forget to consider the type of behaviors that the job holder needs to be able to demonstrate.

At the end of a good interview, you should know which of the expected behaviors are already mastered by the candidate, as well as whether the candidate can be trained and coached to gain mastery on the remaining issues.

Recruit

When interviewing for a role ask plenty of open questions.

6

The questions should be broad enough to offer many possible answers. Don't fall into the trap of unwittingly providing bias or guidance. For example you could ask: "Why did you choose your current job?" and "How closely do you think people should be supervised?" or "What do you enjoy most about selling?"

To be able to compare candidates, also make sure you are consistent in the questions you ask. By structuring your interview, or by having a checklist of topics you will discuss, your recruiting process will become more objective.

Recruit

Focus on strengths, development areas & motivations at shortlist stage in recruitment.

7

Shorten the odds of a successful recruitment campaign by consistently comparing and contrasting candidates. Gather information about motivation & work attitude to plan your second interview or assessment centre. Gain an in depth understanding of how well each person would perform within your culture and which are the strengths, pitfalls and shadow sides.

Recruit

Get a multi-level assessment of a potential recruit!

8

Failed hires are expensive! Have candidates interviewed by three different levels of management in the hiring group. Then send them out to lunch with someone who will be a peer of theirs. Advise the peer to be as open and honest as possible about working here. Then meet and compare perceptions! You will often be shocked at what one or more of the interviewers will report that the other did not see, hear or feel!

Recruit

Learn to hire people virtually!

9

As we move forward into a more virtual world, we must learn how to interview candidates online. It will be even more important to use on-line assessments to support the use of behavioral interviewing approaches where the emphasis will be on truly understanding what they achieved and how they achieved it. Use web conferencing and collaboration tools to be able to use video to watch the interviewee as well to pick up visual cues. Consider using a questionnaire to get an idea about work attitude and motivation, even in a first selection round.

Recruit

Before the first work day, make sure you understand the motivational preferences of the person you have hired.

10

Focus on the two most important 'strengths' and the two most important 'weaknesses' of the person. Keep this in mind during the first day, when you talk to the newly hired person, when you assign tasks, when you ask feedback, etc.

Recruit

Model what is already working in your organization before you hire any new staff.

11

Retraining of the workforce is nowadays a big focus area in organizations due to the expense of hiring and training of new employees and impact of high staff turnover on employee morale.

Companies tend to hire people just for their work experience or for their technical skills instead of appreciating their attitude and motivation. Model your top performers to know truly what it is you want more of in your organization. You will spend less time and money on their development, get them to "hit the floor" and produce results quicker.

Recruit

Know thyself.

12

The team is often a reflection of its leader. Have you been bringing people on the team that you like? Or did you recruit who was needed to make the team perform? Using a team model can take the personal bias out of the equation.

Recruit

All that glitters...is not gold...

13

Have you ever been fooled by job candidates that seem wonderful at the interview and during their first or second month at work but then *poof* they vanish and change into your biggest nightmare? The MBA, Great First Impressions, Answers to Tough Questions, Past Experiences, Job References and other criterion are all important but there's more to look out for. It is those candidates with "the Right Attitude" that set apart the Great from the Good. As the famous saying goes..."Train for Competence, Coach for Performance but always Hire on Attitude!"

Recruit

Listen carefully the answers to your interview questions.

14

Are the candidates' answers providing enough examples of the behaviors and attitude you are looking for in the role? The spontaneous response will be the best indicator of their future behavior. If candidates ask for an explanation, just reply that you are interested in what they mean. Let them know that it is their interpretation of the questions that is important. Let them reveal themselves to you using their own filters and perceptions.

Recruit

Hire tough and you'll manage easy. But hire easy and you'll manage tough.

15

These are the words of Eric Harvey, CEO of WalktheTalk Inc.; a company dedicated to teaching corporations how to create values-driven cultures. If you want to build and develop a world beating culture it always has to start with selection. Trying to change and influence the attitudes and behaviors of competent, but negative people, who were the best candidates on offer, is an uphill battle. Hiring keen and eager people with a 'service first' attitude who need some honing of their skills is always going to pay dividends by comparison - especially in front line, customer-facing roles.

Deploy

The key to productivity is fit.

16

At work, going against the 'grain' is like asking someone to run uphill dragging a spare tire – not productive. Working in alignment with your natural motivations and attitudes is like grabbing that tire and tobogganing down a snow covered mountain to the bottom – effortlessly productive.

Deploy

Act and react in congruence with the profile of the person you hired during their first month of employment.

17

If you think he or she has 'a fitting' profile (otherwise it was a mistake to hire this person), motivate this person based on their profile, by providing the information they need to function, to organize their work and to take decisions. Make sure that you use positive, motivational language whilst doing so.

Deploy

Review the performance of a new member of staff after their first month.

18

Check the person's profile again and see how strengths and weaknesses have played a role during the first month. Adapt the tasks and assignments AND your own management style to the profile of the person you hired.

Deploy

Get results through your people.

19

Do you know what really motivates your people? Find out what it takes to get the job done and assign it to the one who wants it most. Then give them the resources. Magic happens when people use their own wings.

Develop

To make real progress, work with the future in mind.

20

Thinking about yesterday slowed you down, didn't it? Rather than considering what went wrong and who is to blame, figure out what there is to learn so that better results will be obtained in the future. Rather than focusing on a person's weaknesses, consider how work can be organized to make better use of the person's strengths.

Develop

Focus on both the person and the task.

21

Under stress managers may become more task focused and leave people feeling neglected.

Show people that you understand how they feel about changes. Tell them how you feel about things and show you care. Let them know what needs to be achieved and the consequences of both achieving success and what will happen if targets, goals or standards are not met.

Develop

The best way to start a mentoring relationship is to check out the mentee's strengths and preferences.

22

When mentoring a person, you want to help them to deploy their strengths and gain enough self-knowledge so that their dislikes don't get in their way. Listing strengths and preferences forms an excellent basis for an open discussion and certainly accelerates the orientation process.

Develop

Aim to give each professional control over their development.

23

Once an employee has taken the enterprise's recommended basic training and education for their chosen career in their first few years of experience, give them the opportunity to assess and know themselves. Then teach them to manage their own selection of development experiences to best grow themselves professionally within the annual budget allotment for this purpose.

Develop

To truly integrate training and education, teach what you have learned!

24

Once you have completed an investment in a learning experience, follow up afterwards by preparing and delivering a one hour online webinar to an audience of your peers or your network. Teach the essence of what you learned and how it can be used to further the success of what you and they are engaged in professionally. Master the new challenges of doing this in an online world.

Develop

Are you an apprentice, individual contributor, mentor or champion?

25

We move through these four stages of professional development as we master a discipline, use this knowledge to empower others and then become champions of great causes. We can choose to plateau at one of these levels in a given discipline or we can choose to develop through these stages in multiple professional areas (MBA, anyone?)

Inventory your areas of expertise and then assess yourself on this model, bringing great clarity to exactly where you are and where you want to be professionally.

Develop

Create balance between personal life and work.

26

Managers with high levels of emotional intelligence are better at creating balance between their work and their personal life. By developing your EI competencies you can become a whole person with a whole life.

Develop

Remain calm during crises.

27

Remain composed and calm during crises, rely on facts and learn from your mistakes by controlling your emotions and impulses. This will greatly increase your sense of happiness, confidence and greatly reduce stress.

Develop

Learn to deal with change effectively.

28

If you want to be better at implementing strategy, facilitate organization change and overcome resistance to your initiatives you must develop your emotional intelligence. The ability to cooperate and to sustain and build social relationships is essential to success.

Develop

Accept that change is the only constant in business today.

29

Your ability to manage/facilitate change in the workplace is one thing. Your ability to change personally is another thing.

What counts most is your ability to recognize and manage your own feelings first and then those of others in order to produce the results and create profitable business relationships.

The workplace is the ideal environment to develop your social and emotional skills in pursuit of success.

Develop

It is EI and not IQ that determines your level of happiness and success in the workplace.

30

It is not about what qualifications or experience you may have, it is about how you interact with self and others that makes life a happy place to be.

How do you interact with yourself? Can you actually live comfortably within your skin? If you had a choice, would you actually want to live within your own skin?

How you interact with others? Do you treat others the way you want to be treated?

Develop

Attitude can make or break a company, a team or even you.

31

Life is 10% about what happens to us and 90% about how we react to it. We have a choice how we react every day, at every minute or every situation that occurs – we can decide what attitude we embrace that day, that moment, that minute.

We know that it is impossible to change the past; however we can change our attitude about how we deal with the day or the specific situation. So let's learn from the past and apply our learning by changing our attitude.

Develop

When people seem reluctant to look at new ideas, it's often feedback on how you presented your message.

32

People who thrive on alternatives and change will constantly be seeking and coming up with innovations. On the other hand, systems and procedural people who are rooted in the past will instead look to evolve processes and not want to invent them.

You can make change attractive to both types of people just by changing the words you use to fit the profile of the person to whom you're talking.

Develop

If you always feel that you have to defend yourself, be extremely curious as to why!

33

It is quite normal to react immediately if you are confronted with a trait. It is what nature has installed in us. You only will be able to win the discussion more often if your natural reaction would be ...curiosity.

If you ask questions why someone thinks differently to you, you will get a clearer idea of the nature of the misunderstanding or difference.

Develop

Get better at reading non-verbal feedback rather than consistently defending your point of view.

34

If you are a person who needs to be convinced consistently you might use all the arguments you know to get people to understand and agree with your point of view. Since you are not 100% convinced yourself whether you succeeded you keep going on. Look at the faces of the people you are trying to bore into submission, and you'll know when to stop!

Develop

Don't fall in love with concepts at the expense of action.

35

If you are good in concepts you might stay too long conceptualizing. However, more concepts will not get you to go out and do it. You'll just find all the excuses in the world to develop more concepts! So just get out there and get going, set up meetings, and talk to people.

Develop

Focus on improving weaknesses in employees and you will just end up with a bunch of them with strong weaknesses!

36

If you want to develop a high-performing culture do not work on developing people to be more 'well-rounded.' Instead, support your people by focusing on their natural talents and find the right fit for them. Don't waste your time trying to strengthen them in areas that they struggle with. Instead, leverage their innate talents and surround them with colleagues who have complementary talents to match. Aim to create a work environment where everyone can grow and blossom according to his/her own skills and talents.

Develop

"DRH" or "HRD"? Which is your focus?

37

Imagine you are the manager of "HRD." i.e. Human Resource Development. That label says a lot. Immediately you get the feeling that these people for whom you are responsible are merely 'resources' or 'things' to be moved around - just numbers on a page. But they are not. They are your human capital and are the most amazing and potentially powerful resource you have. What if you were to re-title yourself as manager of "DRH"? i.e. Development of Resourceful Humans. Now where is your focus? How might your goals and plans change as a result? That's food for thought.

Evaluate

Never again will you be who you were yesterday.

38

Understand your preferences to be even more successful tomorrow.

Some useful self-evaluation questions:
- If it would depend on you, how would you re-organize your current job to make it better fit what you like?
- If you were free to choose, what would your ideal job be like within your organization?
- If you would be fired, what would your ideal job look like?

Evaluate

Beware the promotion that destroys motivation.

39

When you promote someone make sure you are promoting them based on what they prefer to do rather than what they are just good at. If you promote someone based on skills alone, you could end up killing their motivation and job satisfaction, but promote with motivation in mind and you will have an employee for life.

Evaluate

When people don't seem to get along, map out the conflicting motivational patterns.

40

If you are facilitating a remedial session with two or more people who are experiencing conflict, make a table showing which patterns seem to be at stake. First establish desire to fix the situation (goal), then talk through the issues (reality) and use your table to highlight why conflict is occurring so you can go one to explore options and agree solutions.

Evaluate

Always check the profile of new staff after three months of employment.

41

Evaluation risks being a low priority, especially if deadlines seem to be at stake. Plan a formal evaluation point when a person is three months into their new role. Put this in the agenda and make sure it happens!

Discuss the positives and negatives with the person, list what they like and don't like, analyze it together, and try to find a way to change the negative things into positive behavior. Make a plan together, coach the person.

Evaluate

If a new employee isn't working out after four months, then you need to take action.

42

If you have followed a constant process of re-evaluation of every new member of staff then after four months you will know whether they are going to be valuable to the organization.

If this is not the case, then you have to accept that things may not be working out, and that terminating their employment may well be the best thing to do for all parties concerned.

Evaluate

Get to know yourself better – get in touch with your emotions and feelings before starting to know others.

43

We all deal with other people in the workplace and built relationships wherever we go. The best way to deal with people is to know yourself first. Know who you are and are not. What makes you tick and what doesn't? How you are with other people and how you are not. What your needs and drives are?

By knowing what makes you tick will help you understand what makes you happy and unhappy in the workplace. Knowing this will help you to guide your thinking and actions to those things that will make a difference in your life.

Evaluate

Know the work values that are functioning within your work environment – that of individuals and the different groups.

44

Work values are different for individuals as for groups/teams. These values do not come naturally and have to be cultivated. That is why you can't pay "lip service" to it – you have to "walk-the-talk."

It is not what you as a manager believe your basic work orientation is, whether its people or task values, what really counts is how your followers perceive your behavior.

Evaluate

Can you celebrate small wins or does only the end result count?

45

An example of this is a person involved with laying railway line sleepers punching the air each time one it laid were as his foreman not understanding those and telling him to just get on with it and stop making a fuss as they have 60 miles of sleeper to lay and he doesn't see success or achievement until the total line is laid.

Consider giving positive feedback on a regular basis, even if it's just about some small "details".

Evaluate

The use of motivational & attitudinal patterns in performance coaching is like enabling the DNA of change.

46

We associate DNA with structure. Similarly study your own motivational DNA and enable yourself to use it more explicitly to perform even better in your job and your life. Often better knowing your personal "Motivational Code" enables you to take giant leaps in performance.

Evaluate

Getting to know a person…a 'Whole 9 Yards' better!

47

I have known my cousin for 38 years. It was actually a big surprise for me when I found out things that I never would have known unless I actually worked with him. I am sure you have realized that we are all 'different animals' at work and at play. Some people are also pretty good at masking their actual innate drivers.

Studying the patterns of Work Attitude and Motivation takes the guesswork out of knowing someone whom you have either known for years or just an hour ago…and above all, in the proper work context!

Evaluate

Is there a deeper side of me?

48

I recently met someone who claimed to be "the most profiled girl in the world". So I teased her with the iWAM, as she clearly had not tried it. She was pretty surprised that it showed her many aspects (her motivations and attitudes) that she had not seen with the many other profiles.

It also went on to show that we all have our Extrinsic Traits (seen/known) and the often unspoken Intrinsic Traits (unseen/unknown) that ARE a part of us which, like beauty...is only skin deep. We owe it to ourselves to go beyond to uncover the real beauty within. Priceless.

Evaluate

The case of climbing the corporate ladder...

49

Not everyone can work in a group environment or even share responsibilities (KPIs) with others. Some people are (and will always be) more comfortable being in control of their individual environment and their destiny in solely being responsible for their targets. Imagine if the unsuited people were pushed up to higher positions, it could act as a disservice to them vs. an opportunity to climb the corporate ladder. Track attitudinal preferences of a person in terms of Work Environment and Work Responsibilities to avoid that things turn ugly after a promotion.

Evaluate

Be aware of black and white thinking patterns or perfectionism.

50

How would you detect this pattern in your staff and what implications does it have for the overall effectiveness of how they are motivated? Listen to what they say. Do they discount efforts or outcomes that are less than perfect; do they talk in 'all or nothing' terms? Do they discount incremental effort, change and success?

This pattern of thinking may sabotage the member of staff recognizing that they may, in fact, have made progress when they believe that they have not.

Evaluate

When it comes to 'values violators' you have to draw a line in the sand, regardless of their performance.

51

Jack Welch, ex CEO of General Electric, said it best about the four types of executives in his company. Type 1 deliver the results and believe in our values. They are the role models. Type 2 just do not fit our work ethic and values so need to leave. Type 3 believe in our values but sometimes struggle, so they need to be supported and coached. Type 4 deliver short term, measurable results, but without regard to our values. They 'deliver' while people get hurt in the process. By removing Type 4 executives, our message to our people was clear and our culture flourished.

Retain

Upfront discussion saves a lot of downstream frustration.

52

Before you begin a project or task with someone it is worthwhile asking them how they would like to begin. The answers might surprise you:

a). *I like to work it out as I go.*
b). *I like to understand what we are trying to achieve first.*
c). *I like to structure the various parts before I can begin.*

If their response doesn't match yours, save yourself some frustration and decide how to structure your work together before things get messy!

Retain

Explain the Why as well as the How.

53

More and more people – especially Generation Y – are looking for meaning in their work. If they don't get a good reason for doing something they may not be motivated to do learn it or do it.

Retain

In the offices we deal with people
(We deal with people in businesses.)

54

In the workplace we deal in the first instance with humans and not machines. Human beings are not operated through fuel or electric power but through good relationships.

Having the best strategies, technology or equipment means nothing if people are unhappy in the workplace. We deal with people by building relationships and by taking into account their values and motivations.

Retain

It is the softer skills that make businesses successful today!

55

We know the saying nowadays that it is about working smarter not harder. Autocratic management styles are out and gone are the days that it is all about working harder (whether for the promotion or more production).

Interpersonal effectiveness and building long-term relations with employees and customers is the foundation of long term success.

Retain

Educate your staff on the benefits of 'Continuum Thinking'.

56

A very valuable tool to introduce to staff in order to help them perceive change more positively is 'Continuum Thinking'. This motivational pattern recognizes that changes occur in small increments, adding up to a sustainable outcome.

As a manager, you can assist your staff with this pattern to achieve sustainable change by encouraging them to focus on spotting, documenting, reporting and celebrating incremental changes as, and when, they occur.

Retain

If you are managing staff who are big picture thinkers, but not into detail...

57

These patterns may encourage insight and awareness, but it may also manifest as a lack of awareness of the small, often detailed changes that are occurring within them over a period of time.

Discuss these motivational patterns and alert them to pay attention to the small details that are shifting in their behaviors and feelings. Get them to document and report these changes to you so that you can assist them to validate and sustain such incremental changes.

Retain

Give people new challenges when they need them.

58

Some people may thrive on change and want new challenges quickly. Others prefer their work to remain more stable. But after a while, anyone risks to get bored by their current job.

Make sure to give people new opportunities when they need them, or they might start looking elsewhere...

Retain

Understanding peoples' intrinsic motivation for doing things enables you to help them perform better.

59

When people realize their own motivations better, sometimes they leave the job they're in "And Quickly".

This is not always a bad thing: some organizations pay a fortune to let people go. When people become aware of how their attitude and motivation plays a role, it can enable them to see for themselves how the uphill battle is they're in is just too much, and enable them to find a different career that really suits.

Retain

Most of our behaviors are unconscious reactions. Help others to unravel the underlying causes.

60

Understand why people keep making the same mistakes over and over again by studying their work attitude and motivation to see clearly why they get so stressed around a changing workplace. They will also be able to see how their focus on sameness and place is in the top quartile against the rest of the population, and in this moment they can start to "choose" a change and put in place strategies to worry less about it.

Retain

From Partnership to "Court"-ship.

61

An Entrepreneur complained how a partnership in which he was involved began beautifully but is ending up sour as he is considering bringing his partner to court! Yet the business is not performing badly! It has grown so fast that greed (money) and control (power) has become an issue. Conflicting preferences in Attitude and Motivation can "predict behavior" that could make or break relationships especially when the attitudinal drivers are not aligned with key values of the two parties. Making these preferences explicit can solve the conflict.

Exit

When someone leaves your organization, make sure you do a real exit interview.

62

Exit interviews are a rich source of information to help your organization improve and retain valued employees, because rarely will you receive such frank feedback from current employees.

Remember that the first cause why people leave the organization are linked to "management", so ask about their views about management and leadership, in the organization in general, as well as specific questions about how their direct manager or supervisor could improve their management style and skill.

Exit

When bringing the bad news, focus on the motivational side.

63

When asking a person to leave an organization, often the focus is on the lack of results or the "bad behavior" of the person who is being fired. Instead, consider asking the person whether they really liked doing the job, and discuss which part of the job they didn't seem to like. Point out how their motivation got in their way.

Exit

When helping a person who lost their job, have them focus on their strengths.

64

Try a positive approach, rather than focusing on what went wrong or on development areas. Figure out what motivates the person, what they like doing and what they are good at.

Next, rather than looking too much at "job descriptions" in the "wanted" pages, look to what extent these qualities are appreciated in the job market, and at which organizations these talents are valued.

Exit

Look for a place where the person will fit.

65

Rather than looking for a similar job, or a job in the same industry, look for a job where the competencies and attitude preferences are appreciated. Check whether the organization you want to work for really shares your values, or consider to what degree you want to compromise.

Organizational Culture

Culture is all about values, beliefs and identity!

66

To understand an organizational culture, proactively map out its collective values, beliefs and identity and then share, debate and discuss it to ensure that each person truly understands the culture. Include assessing the predominant behavioral profiles of the organization to allow each member to assess their fit into the culture. This is all too often an eye-opening experience.

Organizational Culture

Why are they asking us to do this?

67

Employees who clearly understand the need for their efforts and how their efforts align with what is truly important to the enterprise are far more motivated to get the job done. Clearly define both the "order" that is driving the work and the "customer" who placed the order. Define and validate the business case for the order with both the "customer" and your superiors. All too often, work often persists beyond the life of the order that requested it.

Organizational Culture

Quickly launch teams by proactively building their cultures!

68

Team culture is one of the most critical factors in team performance especially in today's virtual world where distributed teams are becoming the norm. To do this, collaborate as a team to document a "team operating agreement" which clearly documents how the team will work together in areas such as communication, meeting rules, commitment management, dealing with differences, managing changing requirements and decision-making.

Organizational Culture

Culture is all about behavior, not words on a page or wall.

69

If you want to know the culture of an organization, often the last place to look is its company Vision; Mission; and Values statements. Assess true culture by noticing 'the way we do things around here.' i.e. What is rewarded, punished or condoned? Are there any 'sacred cows'? How did executives rise to their positions? Are there any unspoken rules?

Organizational Culture

It's not enough to just have values or talk values ... you have to do values!

70

Values are a nice set of words which people aspire to 'have.' Like... "We have Honesty; Integrity and Respect as three of our company values." But you can't really have a value as it's an intangible concept. For values to be effective they need to be turned into behaviors. Then we can observe them in action or not. For example..."In our company do our policies treat people with respect? When we do business with our suppliers do we act with integrity?" Only by observing how your organization operates can you discover whether it is actually acting based on its values.

Organizational Culture

Organizations do not change. People change, and then they change organizations.

71

Far too often we hear of the new leader arriving and within a few months that fear-inducing word 're-structure' appears. But does anything really change? Probably in the short-term, but within 2-3 years the people, whose lives were turned upside down, react according to their own patterns and behaviors and the organization finds its own level of performance. So what's the best advice to aspiring CEOs? Just sit tight, ask questions, listen, and do nothing until you really know the beast before you. And the best place to start the dialogue is with your customers, not your direct reports.

Organizational Culture

The real organizational culture mirrors the leaders.

72

Who are the inner circle and what got them there? What are the behaviors of the leadership team?

Attend the executive meetings and observe behaviors around the table. Does the leadership team "walk the talk"? Or does the company values only apply to 'the rest of them' - not 'us' the chosen few?

Organizational Culture

It's simple. Just communicate clearly communicate and listen better!

73

Lack of communication is more than often the number one component highlighted in organizational culture surveys. Most of the time we do all the talking ourselves, and seldom do we ask questions or listen carefully.

You need to ensure that the receiver of the message understands the message the same way you intended to and have the same meaning as you. Therefore ask questions to check understanding and then listen if the same meaning is attached to your intended message as planned.

Organizational Culture

Even the biggest organizations in the World can change their cultures quickly.

74

When we showed team members from one of the largest Oil & Gas organizations in the world what motivators they were driven by, and where this might be a risk to them and their business, they decided to change. To communicate more often, ask more questions and to look to each other more for answers rather than keeping quiet.

Organizational Culture

Analyzing key drivers in your business culture can enable you to show teams their group "Motivational Tendencies".

75

When a group of people understand the keys motivational factors driving them and don't like them, this can provide major "reasons" to change. When this happens often *performance* changes for the better also, and fast!

Team Building

Make teams diverse enough.

76

A leader may need someone who knows it's important to have patience. A go-getter needs someone who will warn for the problems you are likely to encounter.

Team Building

A difference of perspective is a cause for celebration and learning.

77

Each person has a unique way of thinking and acting, seeing through a different set of filters. Rather than confusing "different" with "being wrong' or 'not getting it', try to understand where that person is coming from. For example, on a team it is helpful to have someone focus on the problems, to prevent issues down the track, but often these contributions are considered 'negative'. The next time you get a 'negative' contribution, celebrate the difference in perspective and consider the potential cost you just avoided.

Team Building

Compare the team's motivational & attitudinal preferences annually for greater team harmony.

78

You may want to create an overview of preferences and dislikes of each of the team members. What motivates them? How do they want to organize their work and work environment?

Check this yearly to see how people have changed and adapted to organizational culture as well as highlighting differences and similarities. This is excellent for team harmony and understanding.

Team Building

It is all about flexibility, balance and pace!

79

On the many behavioral spectrums that we all operate, if we have flexibility in how we operate (e.g. proactively versus reactively) then we will best match each other's behaviors and work most effectively as a team. Operating from a balance point in mid-spectrum positions us to best shift and address challenging situations. If we then pace the rate of action appropriately, we ensure no stakeholder is left behind yet the goal is realized in a timely manner.

Team Building

The most flexible system element wins the power!

80

General systems theory teaches us that the most flexible element – (e.g. person, team, etc.) in a system ultimately gains all of the power over the system. Martial arts teaches that "bending with the wind" allows one to maximize one's use of power in a competition.

A truly flexible communicator elegantly matches their audience and gains rapport very quickly and then efficiently influences them. Assess your team members' behavioral profiles and learn how to increase flexibility in everyone's behaviors.

Team Building

Over- communicating is a pretty rare phenomenon!

81

In our globally connected very virtual business economy, communications channels are inexpensive and easily accessed. Using them wisely is another key to success. Study the many different emerging communications, collaboration and networking technologies now available through the Internet (such as the rich offerings from Webex, GoToMeeting, LinkedIn, Google Apps, Windows Live, Facebook, Twitter, Mobile Apps, etc.). Appropriately using each of these in the right context will make a significant difference in team performance.

Team Building

Does your team have the required diversity?

82

Will the mix work? Team members bring unique qualities, values, personality and styles and mixing them in a team is like a bowl of fruit salad. It looks nice but doesn't necessary taste nice. Too much of one thing in the salad and it becomes something different – the same apply to the team. Too much of the same behavior could impact a team negatively and affects it overall effectiveness.

Team Building

Let each team member identify their own preferences and discuss the consequences.

83

Each team member must be aware of the potential negative impact/effects of what they bring into the team – how their styles impact the team.

Part of Emotional Intelligence is the ability to tolerate individual style differences whilst developing each team member to be more flexible in their own styles.

Team Building

Give your team new choices around the kinds of behaviors they can improve.

84

A sales team had great potential, but in the past the majority of them had been convinced automatically when their clients said "No" once to going ahead with a sale. After learning how this was a consequence of their work attitude and motivation, they changed their behavior to ask more questions confirming sales and went from worst "State in the Country" to Number One!

Team Building

"TEAM"...there is still "me" in the word.

85

Even though individuals can work well as a team, there are often key similarities and differences amongst them that stand out. Some of the differences complemented, yet some caused clashes in understanding and communication.

Studying the individual's work attitude and motivation shows how the differences in each of us could bring out the best or the beast in us. The lesson here is whether we would choose to 'celebrate diversity'!

Managing A Team

Every strength has its pitfalls.

86

Some people are good at taking initiative and setting goals. But one might want to move too fast, not taking into account that others need some more time to follow, or need to know how to overcome the problems which will be encountered.

In a balanced team, the pitfalls of some team members are compensated by other team members, provided that the members see the different points of views as enrichment, rather than a source of conflict.

Managing A Team

Be aware of your own personal preferences.

87

It takes a broad range of skills and approaches to make a highly successful team. Ensure that you are not only managing your team in the way you like to be managed. What may seem motivating to you, may not work for all team members.

Managing A Team

Observe and Ask.

88

It is useful to ask your team about the way they like to be managed. i.e. Do they need plenty of feedback and value bouncing ideas off you or do they like making decisions for themselves? Do they like to be responsible of specific goals, or do they prefer to share responsibility with other team members?

Managing A Team

Trust is a critical element of team performance!

89

Especially in today's much more virtual working environments, establishing trust between team members and with their leader is even more of a challenge. To trust someone means that you are completely confident that you know how they will behave in any situation. No surprises! Work as a team to clearly document and share trust factors in the most important areas such as goals, roles, processes, relationships, values and beliefs.

Managing A Team

How to survive a change in team leadership.

90

Team leadership changes can be very disruptive if not managed well. Develop a formal or informal new leader integration process which includes well structured questions to be asked of the new team leader by the team and vice versa. Prior to meeting, have the team build their questions, lists of known issues and challenges and clear statements of what the team knows and what it does not know about the project and the new leader.

Managing A Team

Become a participative manager.

91

Effective managers get buy-in from colleagues at the beginning of an initiative by involving them, engaging them through listening and communicating, and by influencing them in the decision making process. Building your emotional intelligence will make you a better participative manager.

Managing A Team

Put employees at ease.

Make people feel comfortable in your presence by learning to control you impulses and anger. Pay attention to their emotions as well as to what they are actually saying in words. Cultivating your emotional intelligence will boost your own happiness and productivity as well as your employee.

Managing A Team

Handle problematic employees better.

93

There is a direct link between managers' emotional intelligence and their ability to deal with problematic employees.
Being able to express your feelings, viewpoints and beliefs in a constructive way will improve your ability to deal with difficult people at work.

Finding out what motivates the person's "problematic" behavior is a good starting point, in the sense that it can lead to help the person to come to a better way to satisfy the underlying need.

Managing A Team

All super-bosses are leader-managers.

94

Conventional business cultures tend to create good managers, not leaders. That's why managers apply positional power and focus more on the task at hand. On the other hand, the leader relies on personal power and is more people oriented/focused.

Moving from a good manager to a great leader would thus mean developing emotional intelligence skills in interacting with people.

Managing A Team

Credibility and open communication are the key ingredients to leadership success.

95

Credibility is a pre-requisite for any managerial or leadership success. It is built by "walking-the-talk", by doing what you say you will do, by being trustworthy, having integrity and be honest.

Trust is the key component of sound interpersonal relations. Employees and colleagues will trust you if you are reliable, open, and sincere and if you show respect for them.

Managing A Team

Be absolutely clear about who you are and what you stand for (as company, team or individual).

96

We all (hopefully) have values that our company, our team and ourselves stands for. They are not a wish list, but fundamentally and deeply held values that we will "fight" for and seldom change.

Share these values openly with the employees and your team members will create understanding what to expect.

Managing A Team

Recognizing and understanding other opinions helps develop personal rapport (in coaching and mentoring).

97

Showing empathy is a way in being aware and considerate of other people's feelings, opinions and cultural differences.

Empathetic leaders are much more effective in retaining key talent as they built personal rapport with coachees or protégés during the different coaching and mentoring stages/sessions. This also provides unique opportunity for providing feedback to the coachee/protégé which not only improve coach-coachee or mentor-protégé relationships but will buy goodwill which will result in retaining of key talent.

Managing A Team

EQ impacts leadership style which, in turn, impacts overall organizational effectiveness.

98

Research suggests that 50 to 70 percent of employees' perception of working climate is linked to the EQ characteristics of the leader.

It is therefore essential that leaders develop and maintain emotional intelligence skills and continuously measure the impact thereof.

Managing A Team

Perception is as good as self-deception.

99

We know that reality is not always what we think or believe it is. So to perceive that you are the only one that is right might just be the biggest deception.

Never say: *"I am good. They are bad."* You are part of them in the organization.

Focus on what you can contribute to the team and organization and not only on what you can get for yourself.

Managing A Team

If people don't get what you mean, try explaining it again in another way.

100

Some people understand things straight away. Others need more time. Maybe they need to know the whole concept before it clicks with them.

People who don't need that kind of depth already have their own take on it and expect others to click in as fast as they do. Even though it may be frustrating, it is worth taking a deep breath and explaining again or finding another way because the important thing is that everyone properly understands the point you are putting across in whatever style works for them.

Managing A Team

Make your team meeting a place of real people sharing ideas and real emotions.

101

At your next team meeting ask people to select what behavior or quality they appreciate most about themselves. Let them describe in what way this has helped them this week to achieve what they wanted. You will get great stories and the energy in the room is fantastic to use for the rest of the meeting.

Managing A Team

Managing a team is like conducting an orchestra.

102

A good conductor needs to know the nature of sound that each instrument makes and tune each one so that they resonate to each other, making the best use of all.

Mergers & Acquisitions

Most mergers fail to build a more successful enterprise!

103

Merging is a matter of disciplined systems integration! One critical element in a merger is to thoroughly map every life cycle process of managing each and every important enterprise resource. Then ensure that there is only one of each such system survives after the merger. This takes a massive investment of time and energy but the payout is huge! Remember to also include the life cycle of resources such as policies, standards, beliefs and values!

Mergers & Acquisitions

When merging two organizations, consider the impact of the differences in organizational cultures.

104

One culture may be more proactive, goal or task oriented than the other. The values which are important for one organization can be less important to the other one. Depending on which culture prevails, people may feel disoriented, or feel their motivational needs are no longer addressed or worse, that the organization no longer respects their values.

Mergers & Acquisitions

Prevent conflicts in the new organization by creating awareness about the cultural differences.

105

Our preferences and dislikes in terms of Work Attitude and motivation often serve as filters. They determine which part of reality we like seeing and will be paying attention to. They also determine which part of reality we tend to ignore.

Rather than acting upon different preferences as sources of conflict, appreciate how others are different and cherish what they bring to the table: they help to get a more complete view on reality.

Authors

This book is the result of a collective effort of coaches, consultants and trainers who invest a considerable amount of their time to improve emotional intelligence at work. They all have shared a couple of tips they believe in, and which have been making a huge difference in the results they have obtained for themselves, their colleagues or their customers.

We have listed the authors in an alphabetic order:

Sarah Ainsworth, Anneli Blundell, Brian Clark, Jonas Harring Boll, Hunter Dean, David Klaasen, John Lane-Smith, Melvin Leow, Patrick Merlevede, Russ Milland, Seiko Motoyama, Jane Sunley, Wim Thielemans, Peter Van Damme, Dawie van der Merwe, Evelynn Van Mossevelde & Sally Vanson. The contributors come from Australia, Belgium, Canada, Japan, Malaysia, South-Africa, UK & USA

Resources & Further Reading

Other books in this series:

Merlevede, P. & Vurnum, G. (2010): Choose A Career and Discover Your Perfect Job: 105 Tips on Work Attitude and Motivation

See www.jobEQ.com/105Tips

Related Books

Merlevede,P , Bridoux, D. et al (2001): 7 Steps to Emotional Intelligence

Merlevede, P. & Bridoux, D. (2004): Mastering Mentoring & Coaching with Emotional Intelligence

Rose Charvet, S. (1997), Words that Change Minds: Mastering the Language of Influence

Rose Charvet, S. (2010), The Customer is Bothering Me

Instruments

The **Language and Behavior Profile** (LAB Profile) is an interview technique to measure Work Attitude and Motivation.

The **Inventory for Work Attitude and Motivation** (iWAM) is a questionnaire which has been designed to help to discover what motivates a person, which are their strengths and weaknesses, and for which jobs are these qualities best suited. You can test out the iWAM yourself by contacting any of the authors of the book. To see what the iWAM measures, check out the page : **http://www.jobeq.com/categories**

The creation of this book has been made possible by jobEQ.com, the developer of the Inventory for Work Attitude and Motivation.

See
http://www.jobEQ.com/iWAM

"Your Customers And Your Team Are Paying Attention To How You Attract And Treat Them!"

Find out the hidden Motivation Triggers to understand, predict and influence your peoples' behavior.

Two books to help you:

- Decode how your people actually think and make decisions

- Find out the real reasons why organizations mismanage their customers' experience

- Create a Customer Philosophy that gets and keeps customers

- Navigate The Great Customer Attitude Shift

- Enable your people to handle any customer

- Deal with upset customers to create enduring loyalty

- Discover the new rules for mass marketing and direct marketing

- Get your customers to buy more, sooner

Demonstrating you comprehend your people is enormously profitable. Not doing so is hazardous to your corporate health.

Words That Change Minds and *The Customer is Bothering Me*, by international bestselling author Shelle Rose Charvet.

Available in paperback or e-book at your bookstore or from:

www.WordsThatChangeMinds.com

About JobEQ And The iWAM Questionnaire

jobEQ was created to help everyone find "the job of their lives". Our international network of partners helps people to find the right job which fits their attitude and motivation, as well as helping organizations to figure out what are the best motivational and attitudinal patterns for a job, thus creating a better match.

By comparing personal preferences with the ideal profile for a job (based on the patterns of the top performers), we help to get better results in recruiting, training & coaching. We also help managers to motivate people in better ways and help organizations to structure work in a way that motivates their staff more effectively.

Finally, we help organizations to study their organizational cultures, and take this into account when planning large change projects or mergers & acquisitions.

One of the key instruments for matching personal preferences and organizational needs is the iWAM questionnaire, which measures and analyzes in great depth the motivational and attitudinal patterns covered in this book.

If you want to learn more about your own strengths and weaknesses, try out the iWAM for free at: **www.jobEQ.net/SelfTest**

If you or your business are involved in any form of 'human resources management' then discover how jobEQ and the iWAM can help you at: **www.jobEQ.net/joinus**

Made in the USA
Lexington, KY
18 April 2011